U.S. CHEMICAL SAFETY AND HAZARD INVESTIGATION BOARD

INVESTIGATION REPORT

VINYL CHLORIDE MONOMER EXPLOSION

I0502927

(5 Dead, 3 Injured, and Community Evacuated)

FORMOSA PLASTICS CORP.

ILLIOPOLIS, ILLINOIS

APRIL 23, 2004

KEY ISSUES:

- HUMAN FACTORS
- HAZARD EVALUATION
- INCIDENT INVESTIGATION
- EMERGENCY RESPONSE

REPORT NO. 2004-10-I-IL

MARCH 2007

Contents

Figures

Tables

Acronyms and Abbreviations

ACC	American Chemistry Council
AIChE	American Institute of Chemical Engineers
CAA	Clean Air Act
CCPS	Center for Chemical Process Safety
CFR	Code of Federal Regulations
CMA	Chemical Manufacturers Association
CSB	U.S. Chemical Safety and Hazard Investigation Board
IEMA	Illinois Emergency Management Agency
EHS	Environmental, health, and safety
EPA	U.S. Environmental Protection Agency
FPC	Formosa Plastics Corporation
FPG	Formosa Plastics Group
HAP	Hazardous Air Pollutant
IARC	International Agency for Research on Cancer
IEPA	Illinois Environmental Protection Agency
MACT	Maximum Achievable Control Technology
MOC	Management of Change
NESHAP	National Emissions Standard for Hazardous Air Pollutants
NFPA	National Fire Protection Association
NRC	Nuclear Regulatory Commission
OSHA	Occupational Safety and Health Administration
PEL	Permissible Exposure Limit
PHA	Process Hazard Analysis
ppm	parts per million
psi	pounds per square inch
PSM	Process Safety Management (OSHA)
PVC	Polyvinyl Chloride
RMP	Risk Management Program (EPA)
STEL	Short-Term Exposure Limit
VCM	Vinyl Chloride or Vinyl Chloride Monomer

Executive Summary

On April 23, 2004, an explosion and fire at the Formosa Plastics Corporation, Illiopolis, Illinois, (Formosa-IL) polyvinyl chloride (PVC) manufacturing facility killed five and severely injured three workers. The explosion and fire destroyed most of the reactor facility and adjacent warehouse and ignited PVC resins stored in the warehouse. Smoke from the smoldering fire drifted over the local community, and as a precaution, local authorities ordered an evacuation of the community for two days. As of the date of this report, the facility is shut down and has not been rebuilt.

Vinyl chloride monomer (VCM), a highly flammable chemical and known carcinogen and the primary raw material in the PVC manufacturing process, was the fuel for the explosion and initial fire. Formosa-IL used VCM to manufacture PVC resins. Formosa-IL, a wholly owned subsidiary of Formosa Plastics Corporation, USA (FPC USA), bought the Illiopolis facility from Borden Chemical and operated it for approximately two years before the incident.

The U.S. Chemical Safety and Hazard Investigation Board (CSB) determined that this incident occurred when an operator drained a full, heated, and pressurized PVC reactor. The CSB believes that the operator cleaning a nearby reactor likely opened the bottom valve on an operating reactor, releasing its highly flammable contents.

Opening the bottom valve on the operating reactor required bypassing a pressure interlock. The safeguards to prevent bypassing the interlock were insufficient for the high risk associated with this activity. Two similar incidents at FPC USA PVC manufacturing facilities highlight problems with safeguards designed to prevent inadvertent discharge of an operating reactor.

Two operators working with the shift supervisor attempted to manage the release, did not evacuate, and subsequently died. The CSB determined that facility emergency procedures for evacuation were ambiguous and that facility staff had not conducted a large release emergency drill in more than 10 years.

The investigation identified the following root causes:

1. Borden Chemical did not adequately address the potential for human error:

    a) Borden Chemical did not implement 1992 process hazard analysis (PHA) recommendations to change the reactor bottom valve interlock bypass to reduce potential misuse.

    b) In a 1999 PHA, Borden identified severe consequences for opening the reactor bottom valve on an operating reactor, but accepted the interlock, controlled by procedures and training, as a suitable safeguard.

2. Formosa-IL did not adequately address the potential for human error:

    a) After a 2003 incident at FPC USA's Baton Rouge facility, Formosa-IL did not recognize that a similar incident could occur at the Illiopolis facility or take action to prevent it.

    b) Formosa-IL site management did not implement corrective actions identified in the investigation of a similar incident in February 2004 at Formosa-IL.

3. Formosa-IL relied on a written procedure to control a hazard with potentially catastrophic consequences.

The investigation identified the following contributing causes:

1. FPC USA did not have written guidelines for matching safeguards with risk.

2. FPC USA did not have comprehensive written standards managing interlocks at its PVC facilities.

3. FPC USA did not recognize and address common elements among several serious incidents at its PVC facilities.

4. Formosa-IL employees were unprepared for a major VCM release.

This CSB report makes recommendations to Formosa Plastics Corporation; the Vinyl Institute; the

National Fire Protection Association; the U.S. Environmental Protection Agency; and the American

Institute of Chemical Engineers Center for Chemical Process Safety.

1.0 Introduction

1.1 Background

On April 23, 2004, an explosion and fire killed five and seriously injured three workers at the Formosa Plastics Corporation, IL (Formosa-IL) PVC manufacturing facility in Illiopolis, Illinois. The explosion occurred after a large quantity of highly flammable vinyl chloride monomer (VCM) was inadvertently released from a reactor and ignited. The explosion and fire that followed destroyed much of the facility and burned for two days. Local authorities ordered residents within one mile of the facility to evacuate.

1.2 Investigative Process

Investigators from the U.S. Chemical Safety and Hazard Investigation Board (CSB) arrived at the site on April 24, 2004. The CSB worked with officials from Formosa-IL; the Springfield Fire Department; the Springfield Police Department; the Illinois EPA (IEPA); the Occupational Safety and Health Administration (OSHA); the Illinois Emergency Management Agency (IEMA); and other responding agencies to secure the site and preserve evidence. The CSB investigators interviewed more than 80 hourly, management, and corporate employees; examined, photographed, and cataloged damage to the facility (including equipment inside the plant reactor building); tested relevant equipment; researched and analyzed relevant safety codes, standards, and guidelines; and examined company-provided documents. Investigators interviewed local residents to assess community impact.

1.3 PVC and VCM

PVC is a plastic material widely used to fabricate many products including credit cards, clothing, upholstery, pipe, siding, windows, and flooring. PVC is made from VCM, a colorless gas with a mild, sweet odor, which the average person cannot smell at concentrations below hazardous levels.[1] VCM can ignite when its concentration in air is between 3.6 and 33 percent by volume. It has serious short and long-term health effects, described in Appendix D, and is a known human carcinogen.

The Vinyl Institute, a U.S. trade association, represents manufacturers of vinyl, VCM, vinyl additives and modifiers, and vinyl packaging materials. Formosa Plastics Corporation (FPC USA) is a member of the Vinyl Institute.

1.4   Formosa Plastics Corporation (FPC USA)

Formosa-IL and three chemical manufacturing facilities located in Delaware, Louisiana, and Texas are subsidiaries of FPC USA, headquartered in Livingston, New Jersey. FPC USA employs about 2,100 and has annual revenues of nearly $2 billion. FPC USA is part of the Formosa Plastics Group (FPG).[2] FPG is headquartered in Taipei, Taiwan, and traded on the Taiwan Stock Exchange. Total FPG PVC production worldwide exceeds 5.2 billion pounds annually. FPG employs more than 80,000 and reports annual revenues exceeding $37 billion.[3]

FPC USA establishes environmental, health, and safety (EHS) standards (including Process Safety Management, or PSM); collects and tracks incident and near-miss investigations; conducts annual EHS audits; and provides support to FPC USA facilities.

---

[1] The VCM odor threshold for most people is approximately 3,000 parts per million (ppm), 600 times higher than the OSHA Short-Term Exposure Limit (STEL) (a 15-minute time-weighted average concentration that should not be exceeded).

[2] http://www.fpcusa.com/about/index.html (January 2007).

[3] http://www.fpg.com.tw/html/eng/annu.asp (January 2007).

1.5   Borden, Inc.

Borden, Inc. constructed and operated the Illiopolis, IL PVC plant from 1965 until 1987 when it

transferred ownership to Borden Chemicals and Plastics Operating Limited Partnership (Borden

Chemical). Borden Chemical filed for bankruptcy protection in 2001 and sold the Illiopolis PVC plant to

FPC USA in April 2002. In March 2002, just prior to the sale, FPC USA reviewed Borden Chemical's

EHS programs as part of its pre-purchase research. The purpose of the review was to identify potential

regulatory compliance issues and the costs to correct them. This review identified 39 regulatory findings

and 30 observations related to good management practice. None of these findings or observations related

directly to the causes of this incident.

1.6   Formosa-IL PVC Plant

The Formosa-IL PVC plant, bought from Borden Chemical, included a commodity PVC resin process

(PVC1) and a specialty PVC resin process (called "Paste"). These two processes used 24 reactors to

produce up to 400 million pounds of PVC resins per year. The reactor building (Figure 1) housed the two

PVC production areas – PVC1 and Paste. At the time of the incident, Formosa-IL employed 139 (106

hourly and 33 salaried) workers.

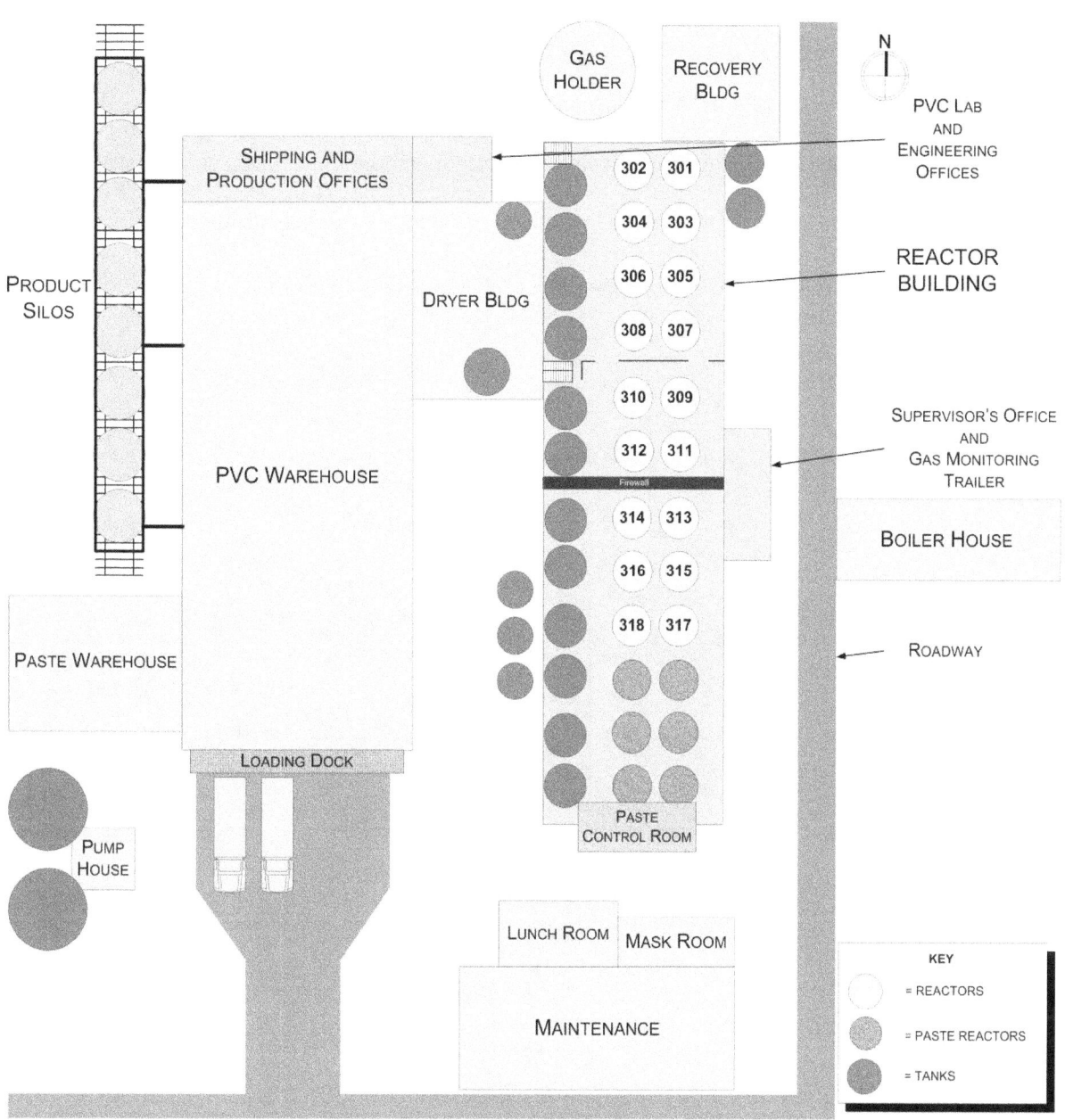

Figure 1. Formosa-IL plant layout

1.7 PVC1 Process

The PVC1 area of the Formosa-IL plant produced PVC by the polymerization of VCM.[4] Liquefied VCM, water, suspending agents, and reaction initiators were reacted in a reactor under heat and pressure. When the reaction finished, the PVC was transferred to equipment to remove residual VCM and to dry, sift, and convey the PVC to storage bins. Figure 2 shows the PVC manufacturing process.

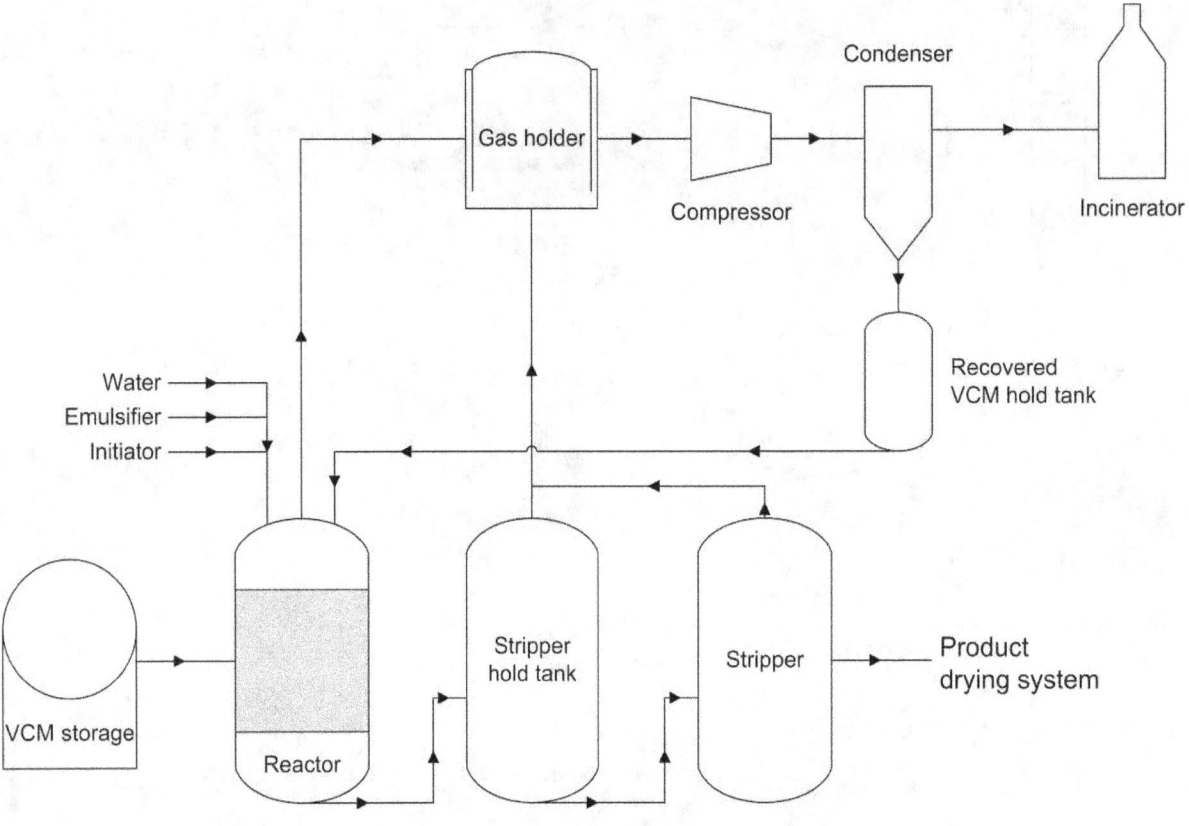

Figure 2. PVC manufacturing process

---

[4] The Formosa-IL PVC1 suspension unit produced both co-polymer and homopolymer resins. Because a homopolymer reactor was involved in the incident, only the homopolymer process is described.

1.7.1   PVC1 Operations

Six operators per shift worked in the PVC1 area where the incident occurred. Two operators, a poly operator and a blaster operator, were responsible for the reactor involved in this incident. The poly operator worked exclusively on the upper level of the building where the reactor controls and indicators were located, while the blaster operator worked on all levels.

Figure 3. Reactor building elevation view

To manufacture a batch of PVC, the poly operator readied the reactor, added the raw materials, and heated the reactor.[5] The poly operator monitored the reactor temperature and pressure until the batch was

---

[5] Temperature was automatically controlled by adding steam or cooling water into the reactor jacket.

complete, then vented pressure from the reactor, and told the blaster operator to transfer the batch to the stripper.

To transfer the batch to the stripper, on the lower level the blaster operator opened the transfer and reactor bottom valves. When the transfer was complete, the blaster operator closed the transfer valve, and the poly operator purged the reactor of hazardous gases to prepare the reactor for cleaning. The blaster operator cleaned the reactor by

- opening the reactor manway,

- power washing PVC residue from the reactor walls, and

- opening the reactor bottom valve (if not left open from the transfer) and drain valve to empty cleaning water to floor drains.

Once the blaster operator finished cleaning the reactor, he closed the reactor bottom and drain valves, and gave the poly operator a completed checklist indicating that the reactor was ready for the next batch of PVC.

1.7.2   Reactor Emergency Procedures

The transformation of VCM into PVC generates heat. If this heat is not removed, an uncontrolled reaction may occur, potentially increasing reactor pressure above the pressure relief device setpoint, venting the reactor contents, including VCM, to the atmosphere.[6] The release of VCM to the atmosphere requires reporting under the U.S. Environmental Protection Agency (EPA) Clean Air Act (CAA) regulations (Section 5.2).

---

[6] A relief device installed on the reactor would open and relieve pressure to the atmosphere to protect the reactor. Each reactor was protected by a rupture disk, then a relief valve relieving to the atmosphere.

Procedures to control reactor overpressure and minimize the possibility of an atmospheric release required that, on abnormally high pressure or temperature, the poly operator would

- manually adjust the reactor temperature control to cool the reactor,

- add a reaction inhibitor to slow or stop the PVC reaction, and

- manually vent pressure from the reactor.

If these steps failed to control the reactor pressure, the operators followed an emergency transfer procedure that required them to open the reactor bottom and transfer valves to connect the reactor to another empty reactor. Borden Chemical created this emergency transfer procedure, concluding that connecting two reactors would promote reaction inhibitor mixing, maximize cooling, and provide extra volume so that the pressure would not exceed the relief device setpoint on the reactor and thereby avoid a reportable VCM release.

1.7.3   Reactor Bottom Valve Interlock

Because opening the reactor bottom valve on an operating reactor could result in a catastrophic release of VCM inside the reactor building, the reactor bottom valve had a safety interlock that prevented opening it with the control switch if reactor pressure exceeded 10 psi.[7]

The emergency transfer procedure, developed by Borden, required that an operator open the reactor bottom and transfer valves to connect the reactor to another reactor. However, during an emergency transfer the reactor pressure is greater than 10 psi and the safety interlock prevents opening the bottom valve. So that operators could open the valve and reduce reactor pressure in an emergency, Borden added an manual interlock bypass. The bypass incorporated quick-connect fittings on air hoses so that operators

---

[7] A reactor pressure transmitter sent a signal to the bottom valve control system. When the pressure was above 10 psi, the control system held the valve closed.

could disconnect the valve actuator from its controller and open the valve by connecting an emergency air hose directly to the actuator.

The emergency transfer procedure required a supervisor to authorize, but not necessarily witness, bypassing the interlock.

1.7.4   VCM Alarm System

The plant had a detection system to monitor airborne VCM concentrations and alert personnel of harmful levels. When the system detected airborne concentrations of one part per million (ppm) (the OSHA permissible exposure limit) or greater, horns sounded and red lights flashed above all area entryways. When the alarm activated, procedures required all personnel in the area to either put on a protective respirator or evacuate.

1.7.5   Deluge System

Formosa-IL and other PVC manufacturers commonly use deluge, or water spray, systems for fire protection and loss control. These systems use water spray nozzles and piping connected to a pressurized water supply to blanket an area with water when activated. The Formosa-IL deluge system was activated by

- high-temperature sensors (for fire detection),

- VCM vapor monitors set at one-half the lower flammability limit for VCM,[8]

- loss of instrument air pressure, or

- manual pull stations located throughout the facility.

---

[8] The lower flammability (or explosive) limit is the lowest concentration of a material, in air, that will propagate a flame.

2.0   Incident Description

2.1   Pre-Incident Activities

Operations at the plant were normal in the hours before the incident. At approximately 10:30 p.m., just moments before the incident, all PVC1 reactors were making PVC except for reactor D306, which was being cleaned.

2.2   Incident

A few minutes after 10:30 p.m., workers throughout the plant heard a very loud rumbling[9] and some smelled VCM.[10] The shift supervisor and operators in the south (Paste) end of the reactor building heard the Paste section deluge alarm, indicating deluge system activation in that area.

The shift supervisor left the Paste control room to check the VCM gas detection system reading. The shift supervisor stated that two areas had levels above the instrument's measurable limit, suggesting a large release. He said that on his way to investigate the release, he walked past an open doorway in the PVC1 area near reactor D310 and saw material spraying from the bottom of D310 and a foaming mixture on the floor about 1.5 feet deep. He immediately climbed the stairs to the upper level.

According to the shift supervisor, operators on the upper level of PVC1 reported that the pressure on the reactor D310 was rapidly falling. He informed two operators that he had seen material spraying from the bottom of D310 and they immediately began checking the valves and controls for D310. The supervisor and one operator tried to go to the lower level through an interior stairwell, but high VCM concentrations forced them to retreat.

---

[9] Some described it as the sound of a jet engine.

[10] The smell of VCM indicated an imminent hazard.

The shift supervisor instructed operators to open vent valves on reactor D310 to relieve pressure and slow the release. At this point, he saw that the reactor pressure had already dropped to 10 psi, further indicating a large release.

Attempting again to go to the lower level, the shift supervisor descended an exterior stairway when a series of explosions occurred.[11] The explosions knocked over two 3,000 gallon VCM recovery tanks; lifted multi-ton dryers off their supports; and destroyed the laboratory, safety, and engineering offices (Figure 1). The ensuing fire spread to the PVC warehouse west of the reactor building, burned for hours, and sent a plume of acrid smoke into the community (Figure 4).

Four operators were killed by the explosions: two working near the top of the reactor and two working on the lower level. A fifth operator died in the hospital two weeks later. The shift supervisor and two workers were hospitalized, and four workers were treated at the scene.

2.3   Incident Aftermath

2.3.1   Community Impact

The fire sent a plume of acrid smoke into the community (Figure 4). In response, emergency responders evacuated approximately 150 residents living within one mile of the plant[12] and the Illinois State Police closed the major roadways in the area.

---

[11] According to witnesses, several explosions followed the initial explosion.

[12] The 2000 Census recorded a population of 916 for the village of Illiopolis. Approximately 70 households—predominately in the Kelsan Heights area of Illiopolis—are located within one mile of the plant; of these, three are within a half-mile.

Figure 4. Smoke plume from the Formosa-IL facility the day after the explosion

2.3.2   Facility Damage

The explosions destroyed much of the plant, blew off the reactor building roof, and tore asbestos-containing paneling and insulation from framing and piping, spreading it across the plant site. The explosions also heavily damaged offices used by day shift employees (Figure 5). As of the issue date of this report, the facility remained closed, and no actions had been taken to rebuild.

Figure 5. Damage to the Safety and Engineering offices

2.3.3   Environmental Impact

After the incident, the IEPA monitored the air and tested water runoff and soil. Both Formosa-IL's contractor and IEPA conducted on- and off-site sampling to test for hazardous substances.[13]

Results from on-site samples indicated the need for continued remedial activities and monitoring to ensure that the site presented no hazard to the community or local environment. According to IEPA and Formosa documents, none of the off-site sampling revealed concentrations of hazardous substances that would concern public health or the environment. Some off-site soil sampling revealed dioxin levels slightly above suggested background level of 1.0 part per trillion (EPA, 2003), but none were at or above the action level of 1.0 part per billion (ATSDR, 1997).[14] As of the issue date of this report, IEPA continues site monitoring and has issued four "Community Relations Fact Sheets."[15]

3.0 Most Likely Incident Scenario

The CSB used physical evidence and survivor interviews to determine the most likely incident scenario. Employee interviews and day shift records indicate that at the time of the incident, reactor D310 was operating with a reaction in process. Reactor D310 was found empty with the reactor bottom and drain valves open, and both valve switches in the "Open" position (Figure 6).

---

[13] IEPA established a public repository for site-related information at the Illiopolis/Niantic Public Library District at Sixth and Mary Streets in Illiopolis, which contains reports related to the investigation and monitoring and cleanup.

[14] These results were for 2,3,7,8-tetrachlorodibenzo-p-dioxin (TCDD).

[15] www.epa.state.il.us/community-relations/fact-sheets/formosa-plastics/, November 2006.

Figure 6. Reactor D310 bottom valve control panel as found after the explosion

The as-found condition of Reactor D306 indicated that it was being cleaned: the top manway was open, the pressure washer was inside, the bottom valve was open, and the drain and transfer valves were closed. The next cleaning step that the blaster operator would have performed would be to open the drain valve and empty the reactor.

Because of the as-found condition of reactors D306 and D310, the CSB concluded that the blaster operator cleaning reactor D306 likely went to D310 by mistake and tried to open the bottom valve to empty the reactor. The D310 valve would not open, however, because the reactor was operating with the pressure interlock activated.[16] Because he likely thought he was at the correct reactor (D306), the blaster operator may have believed that the bottom valve on D310 was not functioning. The CSB concluded that because the bottom valve actuator air hoses were found disconnected and the emergency air hose used to bypass the interlock was found connected, the blaster operator, who likely believed the reactor contained

---

[16] Plant personnel estimate that the pressure inside D310 was approximately 70 psig when the interlock was overridden.

only cleaning water, used the emergency air hose to bypass the bottom valve pressure interlock and open the reactor bottom valve while the reactor was operating, releasing the contents.

The shift supervisor stated that the blaster operator did not request permission to bypass the interlock (required by procedure) or inform anyone that he had bypassed it. [17] Consequently, operators attempting to control the release likely believed that a failure or other malfunction had occurred and tried to relieve the pressure inside the reactor to slow the release.[18] The VCM vapor cloud ignited and exploded while the operators were working at the reactor controls.

4.0   Incident Analysis

4.1   Minimizing Human Error

On April 23, 2004, an operator at Formosa-IL erred when he dumped the contents of an operating PVC reactor by opening the wrong valve. Studies show that human error is a large contributor to fatalities, injuries, and property damage in the chemical industry (CCPS, 1994): "there is a belief…that human error is both inevitable and unpredictable. However, human error is inevitable only if people are placed in situations that emphasize human weaknesses and that do not support human strengths" (Anderson, 1999).

At Formosa-IL, several factors combined to make the human error in this incident more likely. Companies need to evaluate factors that alone do not create high-risk situations, but combined, make human error more likely.

---

[17] The blaster operator was fatally injured when the VCM vapor ignited.

[18] Approximately 15,000 pounds of VCM was released, along with water, PVC, and other reaction ingredients.

4.1.1   Reactor Layout

At Formosa-IL, the PVC1 reactors were arranged in groups of four, with a control panel for every two reactors. Both reactors (D306 and D310) involved in this incident occupied the same relative position among groups of four reactors (Figure 7).

Figure 7. Cutaway of reactor building

Reactor bottom and drain valve control panels were on the lower level. Each reactor was labeled with the reactor number. The control panels, also labeled with the reactor number, had clearly labeled indicator lamps showing the bottom and drain valve positions.

Similar equipment layouts are common in the chemical industry and can create a possibility for human error, which a comprehensive hazard analysis should address (Section 4.3).

4.1.2   Communications

Operators working on the lower level had no means to communicate with operators on the upper level who had ready access to reactor status information.[19] Consequently, an operator at the valve control panel on the lower level, who questioned why a bottom valve would not open, would have to climb the stairs to the upper level to determine reactor status. This "inconvenience" may have contributed to a scenario in which the blaster operator might guess reactor status instead of climbing the stairs to get the status.

The CSB learned that operators at Formosa's Baton Rouge, Delaware City, and Point Comfort plants either carry radios or have access to an intercom system on the lower level.

4.1.3   Staffing Changes

When FPC USA bought the Borden facility in 2002, management reorganized and reduced staff. Interviews and documents obtained by the CSB investigators indicate that when considering what changes to make, FPC USA compared similar Formosa plant sites and Formosa operating philosophy, but conducted no formal managerial or human resource analysis of the staffing changes.[20] These changes, described below, occurred on the day Formosa-IL took ownership of the plant.

Borden Chemical had assigned operators and a group leader (a working supervisor) for each area (such as PVC1). The group leader was an hourly employee responsible for supporting the operators in his/her area. Employees interviewed indicated that the group leader, a respected position at the Illiopolis facility, had an elevated level of responsibility. If an operator had a problem, the group leader for the area was skilled and readily available. For example, if a problem occurred that required that the reactor bottom

---

[19] At Formosa-IL, radios were available, however operators did not normally carry them.

[20] Management of Change (MOC) programs evaluate the safety consequences of changes to facilities that affect a covered process. The OSHA PSM standard requires companies that handle highly hazardous chemical processes to have MOC programs. Since 1989, CCPS has advocated applying MOC to organizational and staffing changes (CCPS, 1989).

valve safety interlock be bypassed, the PVC1 group leader had the knowledge of how, and more important, under what circumstances it could be done. Furthermore, the group leader could usually obtain the shift supervisor's permission to bypass the interlock.

FPC USA management eliminated the group leaders when it bought the facility. Consequently, instead of each operational area having a group leader, a single shift supervisor was responsible for the entire plant. In an emergency, or if an operator needed non-emergency advice or assistance, the shift supervisor might not be as available as the previous group leaders.

Because a shift supervisor might be unable to respond quickly, Borden Chemical, and subsequently Formosa-IL, required only that the supervisor authorize, but not actually witness, the override of the controls for the reactor bottom valve interlock.[21] This lack of availability, combined with communication difficulties (Section 4.2.2) and that the use of the safety interlock bypass would be undetectable, increased the likelihood that an operator might act independently and may have contributed to the unauthorized safety interlock bypass use in both the February 2004 and April 2004 incidents.

4.2   Learning from Incidents

Prior to the April 23, 2004, Formosa-IL incident, both the FPC USA Baton Rouge and Formosa-IL facilities had operators mistakenly open a reactor bottom valve. The FPC USA EHS group had received reports of both incidents, but did not recognize a key similarity: operators could mistakenly go to the wrong reactor and bypass safeguards to open a reactor bottom valve. The following sections describe these incidents.

---

[21] Borden Chemical recognized this was a problem and recommended in the 1992 PHA that the shift supervisor actually witness the bypass. The CSB was unable to determine how Borden Chemical addressed this recommendation.

4.2.1   Baton Rouge 2003 Incident

In June 2003, at Formosa's Baton Rouge facility, about 8,000 pounds of VCM were released when an operator cleaning a reactor mistakenly opened the bottom valve and blind flange on an operating reactor.[22]

This incident was similar to the fatal incident at Formosa-IL, as the operator opened the top manway on the reactor to be cleaned and then went to the lower level, where he mistakenly went to an adjacent reactor, removed a bolted flange cover, and opened a motor-operated drain valve, emptying the reactor contents onto the floor. The operator tried unsuccessfully to close the valve, then evacuated and notified the supervisor. The supervisor immediately switched the valve operation to "Remote" and closed the valve from the control room.[23] In this incident the VCM dispersed without igniting.

The Formosa investigation team could not determine why the operator went to the wrong reactor, as both reactors and the drain valve controls were labeled and the operating reactor agitator could be heard. Since this incident, all reactor drain valves at the Baton Rouge facility are locked when not in use, and only supervisors have access to the keys.

4.2.2   Formosa-IL February 2004 Incident

At Formosa-IL, about 60 days prior to the April 23, 2004, fatal incident, an operator mistakenly transferred the contents of an operating reactor to a stripper tank. Consequently, pressure in the stripper tank exceeded its relief device setpoint and VCM released through the vent pipe to the atmosphere.

Formosa-IL investigated this incident. As in the fatal incident, an operator used the emergency air hose to bypass the reactor bottom valve interlock without supervisor authorization. In response, Formosa-IL

---

[22] The operation at Baton Rouge was different than at Illiopolis: reactors were not cleaned after each batch and the reactor bottom drain was closed with an 8-inch motor-operated drain valve and a bolted cover.

[23] At Formosa-IL the reactor bottom valve can only be operated on the lower level under the reactor.

retrained the operators on emergency reactor transfer procedures, including the requirement for
supervisory approval prior to use of the emergency air hose.[24] In addition, the investigation report
recommended redesigning the interlock bypass to prevent unauthorized use, and established a deadline of
April 1, 2004, for completion.

Employee interviews indicated that Formosa-IL personnel met several times to discuss a new bypass
design, but were unable to agree on one. Formosa-IL personnel continued discussions after the April 1
deadline, but had not implemented any design changes before the April 23, 2004, incident.

4.2.3   Delaware City 2005 Incident

In May 2005, Formosa's Delaware City facility had an incident when an operator mistakenly transferred
the contents of an operating reactor, resulting in a VCM release of about 2,500 pounds. The reactor
bottom valve on all reactors had been chain-locked with two locks to prevent inadvertent operation; one
key was held by the cleaning operator, and the other by the control room operator. On the day of the
incident, the control room operator gave his/her key to the cleaning operator in the control room[25] who
went to the wrong reactor, unlocked both valves, and transferred the contents of the operating reactor.

4.2.4   Other PVC Incidents

Table 1, adapted from *The Encyclopedia of PVC* (Nash, 1986), lists PVC manufacturing incidents similar
to the April 23 Formosa-IL incident in that they include operators going to wrong reactors and opening
bottom valves. These incidents demonstrate that inadvertently draining a reactor is a serious hazard in the
PVC manufacturing process.

---

[24] Records were unavailable to determine if the blaster operator on duty the night of April 23 received this training.

[25] The policy required the control room operator to hand over his/her key in the control room so that the control
room was always attended by an operator.

Table 1. PVC Manufacturing accidents involving inadvertent reactor discharge

Year	Place	Cause	Result
1961	Japan	Contents of wrong reactor discharged.	Four killed, eight injured in plant and two outside. Major structural damage to the plant.
1966	New Jersey	Operator opened wrong reactor bottom valve, discharging contents.	One killed. Plant destroyed.
1980	Massachusetts	Operator opened wrong bottom valve, discharging fresh batch.	Two injured; damage over $1 million.
1980	California	Improper valve design allowed a bottom valve to remain partially open.	Major damage to the plant.

4.2.5   FPC USA Review of Similar Incidents

Investigations of incidents provide valuable opportunities to identify and correct hazards. Both the 2003 Baton Rouge and February 2004 Formosa-IL incidents and three of the incidents in Table 1 illustrate that an operator can mistakenly go to the wrong reactor and open a bottom valve. Moreover, the February 2004 incident illustrates that easily defeated safeguards may do little to prevent operator error. These incidents were warnings of the vulnerabilities that led to the April 2004 fatal incident.

Neither Formosa-IL management nor FPC USA corporate safety personnel recognized common elements of the 2003 Baton Rouge and February 2004 Formosa-IL incidents. In particular, Formosa-IL managers were notified of the Baton Rouge incident, but took no action because they believed the operations were dissimilar, as Baton Rouge did not have an interlock on the reactor bottom valve. Additionally, when the Formosa-IL managers reviewed the February 2004 Formosa-IL incident, they did not act urgently to implement rigorous safeguards to prevent recurrence. The CSB concluded that FPC USA corporate safety personnel and Formosa-IL managers should have recognized the similarities in these incidents, specifically the possibility that an operator might mistakenly open the wrong reactor bottom valve, and made the installation of a more effective interlock an urgent priority.

The May 2005 Delaware City incident further illustrates that more than one year after the Formosa-IL fatal incident, FPC USA corporate safety personnel continued to underestimate the urgency and importance of implementing rigorous safeguards to prevent an operator from opening a reactor bottom valve on an operating reactor.

Companies with a learning culture purposefully study problems such as those revealed in incident investigations, and quickly make changes to improve systems (Hopkins, 2005). This includes reviewing incidents across the corporation, recognizing similar patterns, and ensuring that all facilities take appropriate corrective actions. The FPC USA incident investigation program did not effectively evaluate incidents and communicate findings that could have prevented this incident.

4.3   Analyzing High-Consequence Hazards

One tool for evaluating and protecting against human error is a process hazard analysis (PHA). A typical PHA identifies and evaluates specific process hazard scenarios, including human error, to determine potential consequences. Safeguards[26] are then matched with hazards, and, where gaps exist, a recommendation is issued. The OSHA PSM standard (29 CFR 1910.129) requires facilities using highly hazardous chemicals to conduct a PHA and revalidate it at least every five years, sooner if the process changes significantly.

Borden Chemical completed a PHA on the PVC1 unit in 1992 and a partial revalidation of the PHA in 1999. Formosa-IL had not revalidated the 1999 PHA or conducted a new PHA prior to the April 23, 2004, incident.

---

[26] A safeguard is "any device, system, or action that either would likely interrupt the chain of events following an initiating event or mitigate the consequences" (CCPS, 2001).

4.3.1   1992 PHA

The April 23, 2004, fire destroyed much of the 1992 Borden PHA documentation. What remained verified that the PHA team analyzed the reactor emergency transfer procedure and recommended

- modifying the plant-wide philosophy "to require that no plant interlock be defeated without direct hands-on approval and witnessing of operating supervision"[27] and

- replacing the emergency air hose system with one that required a supervisor's key to override it.

These recommendations, which addressed some key deficiencies that the CSB concluded contributed to the unauthorized use of the bottom valve interlock bypass on April 23, 2004, were never implemented. In addition, site management continued to require that employees obtain only the supervisor's verbal authorization to bypass the reactor bottom valve control.

4.3.2   1999 PHA Revalidation

In 1999, Borden Chemical conducted the partial PHA revalidation of the PVC1 process that included the D310 reactor. The PHA team addressed a previous incident where the contents of an operating reactor were inadvertently transferred, a scenario very similar to what occurred during the February 2004 incident (Section 4.2.2). The PHA team identified potentially severe consequences of fire, injury, and environmental and/or offsite impact, but accepted the existing bottom valve safety interlock, procedures, and training as suitable safeguards.

Inadvertently transferring the contents of an operating reactor was identified as a high-consequence event with a significant likelihood of occurrence (it had occurred at least once). Operating procedures are typically viewed as less reliable safeguards for high-consequence events (Bird and Germaine, 1985), yet

---

[27] Formosa's policy at the time of the incident required that a supervisor authorize the override instead of being present and directly involved.

the safeguards accepted for this high-consequence event were written procedures and an interlock with a bypass controlled only by procedure (the emergency transfer procedure). Such administrative protections may be inappropriate as the sole protection against hazards with severe consequences such as fire, injury, or environmental release of a toxic substance.

4.3.3   Reactor Cleaning Procedure PHA

The CSB investigators noted that neither PHA addressed reactor cleaning procedures. Addressing the reactor cleaning procedure in a formal PHA[28] may have identified the potential for an operator to go to the wrong reactor during the cleaning process, and might have prompted Borden Chemical to implement more rigorous safeguards, like a key lock system, to ensure that operators could not accidentally open the bottom valve on an operating reactor.

4.3.4   Risk Assessment

After identifying likelihood and severity of identified hazards, risk should be assessed to determine if existing safeguards are adequate. Risk, a function of likelihood and severity, is highest when the most severe consequences have a likelihood of occurring frequently (Figure 8). These risks require a higher level of safeguard.

---

[28] The CCPS *Guidelines for Hazard Evaluation Procedures* suggests performing PHAs on procedures for batch processes like that used at Formosa-IL and include a worked example for a PVC production facility (CCPS 1992).

RISK MATRIX – EMPLOYEE SAFETY

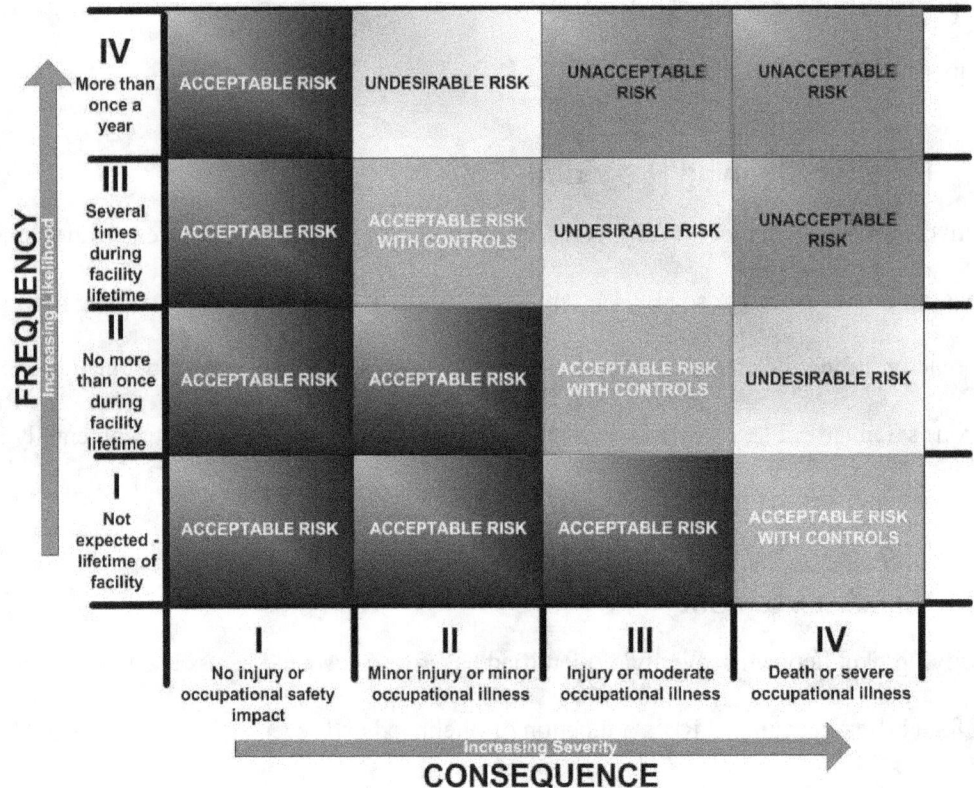

Figure 8. Sample risk matrix for employee safety

Borden Chemical and Formosa-IL used a qualitative approach to evaluate hazards and assess risk for PHAs. A qualitative PHA is conducted by a team of knowledgeable and experienced individuals who identify hazards and review risks to assess the adequacy of safeguards. The team uses experience and judgment to assess a hazard's severity and likelihood, and makes recommendations for additional safeguards when the risk associated with the hazard is perceived to be too high. Relying solely on judgment without standards or written guidance can lead to accepting or specifying an inadequate safeguard for an unacceptable risk.[29] For example, in the 1999 Borden Chemical PHA revalidation, the PHA team identified the high-risk scenario of transferring the contents of an operating reactor, but accepted weak administrative safeguards as adequate to control the risk (Section 4.3.2).

While qualitative approaches to hazard analyses are common in the chemical industry, the Center for Chemical Process Safety (CCPS) has recently promoted a semi-quantitative method called Layer of Protection Analysis (LOPA). LOPA is a more rigorous approach to determine if safeguards are sufficient to adequately control risks in hazardous systems such as chemical reactors. According to the CCPS, LOPA methods have

- a method for classifying consequences,

- criteria for determining risk tolerance (including upper management approval),

- a scenario development procedure,

- rules for considering independence of safeguards,

- procedures for calculating risk, and

- procedures to determine if risk is adequately safeguarded (CCPS, 2001).

In this case, LOPA could be used to determine

- if the reactor bottom valve interlock qualifies as an independent protection layer (IPL), a safeguard whose effectiveness can be measured and audited; and

- if the effectiveness of all combined IPLs is adequate to control risk.

---

[29] Formosa PHA procedures include written guidelines for risk assessment. However, the guidelines are not used to determine if a recommendation should be made, but to prioritize recommendations once they have been made.

A reactor bottom valve interlock LOPA would likely identify that an easily used, poorly controlled, untraceable bypass mechanism would disqualify the interlock as an IPL. Additionally, since LOPA does not accept procedures to be IPLs, the procedural requirement that a supervisor authorize the use of the interlock bypass would not likely qualify.[30] The absence of any other IPL on the reactor bottom valve would likely lead to the conclusion that the risk of inadvertently opening the valve is inadequately controlled and that more robust safeguards are necessary.

4.4 Bypass Control

Formosa-IL management relied on the reactor bottom valve interlock as a key safeguard to protect against accidental transfer or dumping of the contents of an operating reactor, even though the interlock could be easily bypassed. In addition to the reactor bottom valve interlock, the CSB identified other safety equipment that could be easily bypassed:

- Wooden blocks used to prevent inadvertent activation of the deluge system during maintenance hung from each riser valve. Facility management intended that authorized personnel use the blocks only during maintenance; however, because the use of the blocks was uncontrolled, they were vulnerable to misuse, such as not being removed after maintenance.

- A toggle switch installed to disable the VCM gas detection system and prevent automatic activation of the deluge system during maintenance. Other than the switch position, no other indication existed to alert personnel that the system was disabled.

---

[30] Procedures help improve human performance, but because they are not independent of that performance, they are not considered to be IPLs.

4.4.1   Design

The design of a bypass must be highly reliable, effective, and secure. The Formosa-IL bypasses all lacked physical controls needed to make them secure, in that anyone could access and use the bypasses. In addition, failure to provide indication of the bypass condition meant that the condition could be undetected, compromising the effectiveness of the safety equipment.

4.4.2   Policies

Although Formosa-IL had a specific procedure for using the emergency air supply to bypass the bottom valve interlock, the procedure did not include recognized and generally accepted good practices for controlling safety interlocks. The 1992 Borden PHA recommended a "plant-wide" philosophy for controlling interlocks; however, none was implemented at the time of the April 23, 2004, incident.

The CCPS offers best practice guidance for bypassing interlocks:

- Implement a formal facility policy for bypassing interlocks; and

- Write and implement procedures that require

  - process monitoring while the interlock is bypassed,

  - analysis of the appropriateness of the bypass method,

  - a time limit for bypass, and

  - documentation for and communication to all affected personnel (CCPS, 1993).

In addition, *Loss Prevention in the Process Industries* (Lees, 1996) recommends supplementing bypass procedures with additional security measures such as keyed switches or passwords.

Following the April 23, 2004, incident, Formosa's Baton Rouge, Delaware City, and Point Comfort management all instituted site-wide policies for controlling interlocks bypasses.[31] These policies require a manager's signature on a written permit, identification of alternate safeguards to ensure ongoing operational safety, and re-evaluation of bypassed interlocks every 24 hours. A site-wide interlock bypass policy like this, combined with appropriate physical or engineering control over the emergency air hoses, would likely have prevented the April 2004 fatal incident.

4.5   Emergency Preparedness

Worker actions during this incident demonstrate that they were poorly prepared for a catastrophic release of VCM. For example, facility emergency response procedures contained conflicting requirements, workers tasked with critical response duties had not received requisite training, and the workers had not rehearsed a response to a large VCM release in more than 10 years.

The supervisor went to where two operators were trying to control the release rather than call for an evacuation. The CSB estimates that the operators continued their work until the explosion occurred, up to five minutes after the release started.[32] Despite knowingly working directly over a toxic VCM cloud, the operators did not put on protective breathing apparatus, activate emergency alarms, or evacuate the facility, contrary to emergency response actions outlined in Formosa-IL procedures addressing emergency response to hazardous material releases.

The OSHA Hazardous Waste Operations and Emergency Response (HAZWOPER) standard[33] states that employers have two choices when responding to uncontrollable hazardous material releases: they can

---

[31] Prior to the April 2004 incident, FPC USA only required its PVC facilities to institute policies for interlock override as part of a work permit process used for maintenance.

[32] Estimates range from 2.5 to 5 minutes as the time from the start of the release until ignition.

[33] 29 CFR 1910.120.

respond if they are trained and equipped by implementing the rigorous emergency response requirements of the standard, or evacuate to a safe distance and rely on an outside response agency (the local fire or HAZMAT department).[34] Formosa personnel did not evacuate to a safe location, and while they did respond to the release and try to control it, they did not implement the HAZWOPER emergency response requirements.

Formosa-IL managers told the CSB that, in their opinion, HAZWOPER did not apply to the operations of the plant, yet various sections within the facility procedures outline response actions that trigger HAZWOPER requirements by directing employees to mitigate a release.

The Formosa-IL facility had six different procedures relating to VCM release emergencies, which made determining Formosa's plan for responding to a large VCM release difficult. For example, one procedure stated that a trained emergency brigade would respond to releases of less than 55 gallons. Another directed the shift supervisor and unit operators (not necessarily trained in emergency response) to put on protective equipment and take necessary actions to stop a release, yet it did not define the size of the release that employees were to respond to. These ambiguities created uncertainties that increased stress and compounded the potential for mistakes. Given that the procedures outlined employee response actions and that employees did respond to control the VCM release, the CSB concluded that the employees would have been better prepared to respond to this emergency if Formosa-IL had fully implemented the HAZWOPER emergency response requirements.

HAZWOPER training conducted by experienced and qualified instructors, combined with annual refresher training and drills, can help workers handle the stress and emotions experienced during

---

[34] 29 CFR 1910.120(q) exempts an employer from HAZWOPER requirements if employees evacuate from the danger area and do not handle release emergencies and the employer develops an emergency action plan that complies with 29 CFR 1910.38.

emergencies. The shift supervisor and operators who tried to control the release were not trained to the appropriate HAZWOPER emergency response requirements. [35]

The purpose of drills and exercises is to rehearse and test the adequacy of emergency response plans, facility equipment and resources, and employee training and readiness. Drills also help employees realize that hazards are real and understand what actions they should take in an emergency.

The CCPS recommends that emergency response plans specify the type and frequency of drills and exercises, and contain procedures for organizing, conducting, and evaluating them. Furthermore, the CCPS suggests annually conducting a "full scale" exercise and periodic credible incident scenario drills for each process (CCPS, 1995b). Formosa-IL had no written requirements or procedures for conducting drills or exercises; instead of planning exercises or drills, the facility only documented actual occurrences (false alarms, minor system upsets and releases, employee evacuations) and after such occurrences, conducted "lessons learned" sessions with management and employee representatives. Contrary to these recommendations, the CSB found that the Illiopolis facility had not conducted a drill of a large release scenario in more than 10 years.

4.6   Designing Deluge Systems to Prevent Fires and Explosions

Deluge systems can sometimes prevent vapor cloud fires and explosions through several mechanisms:

- Dispersing vapor and inducing air flow into the release, ultimately reducing the vapor concentration below the lower flammable limit (CCPS, 2003).

- Absorbing the substance released; this, however, depends on the properties of the substance, primarily its solubility in water (CCPS, 2003).

---

[35] See CFR 1910.120 (q)(6)for emergency response training requirements for.

- Cooling and condensing vapors from materials with high boiling point temperatures, which may also reduce the vapor concentration below its lower flammability limit (NFPA, 2001).

- Preventing ignition by reducing the potential for static electricity-generated sparks, and by cooling hot surfaces (NFPA, 2001).[36]

Formosa-IL employees believed that the reactor building water deluge system would prevent or mitigate an explosion or fire from a major VCM release.[37]

The PVC1 deluge system did not activate during the April 2004 fatal incident. The CSB was unable to determine a cause for the malfunction. However, the CSB concluded that the PVC1 deluge system would probably not have prevented the fire and explosion by reducing the vapor concentration below the lower flammable limit because

- the PVC1 building was enclosed, thereby preventing effective dispersion of VCM vapors;

- VCM is only slightly soluble in water, making water sprays ineffective for absorbing VCM releases; and

- VCM vapors cannot be condensed by water sprays due to the low VCM atmospheric boiling point.[38]

The CCPS (1997) provides some general guidelines for the design of deluge (water spray) systems for air entrainment, and suggests a strategy for designing a system to mitigate flammable material releases that requires concise definition of the protection scenario. However, the CCPS refers to NFPA 15, *Standard*

---

[36] If electrical components are not sealed properly, water ingress can actually create ignition sources by causing sparks from electrical short circuits (Thomas, 2000).

[37] The CSB collected information on the PVC industry through an informal sampling of PVC manufacturers and learned that other PVC industry personnel have similar expectations.

[38] The boiling point of VCM is -13.6°C.

for Water Spray Fixed Systems for Fire Protection (NFPA, 2001), for specific critical design features of fixed water spray systems.[39]

NFPA 15 states that preventing fire is a legitimate design objective for water spray systems. The standard also provides specific, quantitative guidance on designing fixed water spray systems to extinguish and control burning and for exposure protection. However, NFPA 15 does not provide a clear strategy or detailed guidelines on how to design systems to prevent flammable vapor fires, nor does it include information on, or discussion of, the limitations of such systems. The CSB concluded that more comprehensive and detailed guidance would help manufacturers specify and understand the limitations of deluge systems to prevent flammable vapor fires and explosions.

4.7   Identifying Hazards at Newly Acquired Facilities

Company mergers and acquisitions are common in the chemical industry. The PVC1 process was constructed and operated by Borden, Inc., and when FPC USA bought Formosa-IL, it inherited a design and procedures that presented significant risk, which FPC USA audits did not reveal.

Little industry guidance is available to help companies evaluate process safety risks associated with acquisitions. At least one company, Air Products and Chemicals, Inc., has published an article detailing its corporate program for preventing incidents at newly acquired facilities (Dunbobbin, 2006). However, more industry guidance could assist companies, like FPC USA, develop programs to quickly identify and mitigate risk in newly acquired facilities.

---

[39] NFPA 15 Chapter 7, Section 7.5 contains design objectives for fixed water spray systems (NFPA, 2001).

5.0 Regulatory Analysis

VCM is regulated under OSHA standards 29 CFR 1910.107 *Vinyl Chloride* and 29 CFR 1910.119

Process Safety Management of Highly Hazardous Chemicals (PSM).[40] VCM is also regulated by the

EPA as a Hazardous Air Pollutant (HAP) and under 40 CFR 68 *Risk Management Program.*

5.1 OSHA Regulations

OSHA enforcement in Illinois is generally in response to accidents and complaints, or as part of a targeted

(planned) inspection. During the five years prior to this incident, OSHA conducted no compliance or

enforcement visits to Formosa-IL.

5.1.1 Process Safety Management of Highly Hazardous Chemicals

The OSHA PSM standard provides a structure to systematically approach process safety and catastrophic

incident prevention. It applies to processes containing threshold quantities of specific highly hazardous

chemicals and flammable liquids and gases in quantities greater than 10,000 pounds. The PSM standard

applies to the Formosa-IL facility because Formosa-IL stored and used VCM and vinyl acetate in

quantities greater than 10,000 pounds.[41]

PSM-covered processes require adherence to 14 good safety management elements. The elements most

relevant to the root and contributing causes of this incident are

- Process Hazard Analysis—1910.119(e). (Section 4.3);

- Management of Change—1910.119(l). (Section 4.1.3);

---

[40] Because the process at Formosa-IL contained more than 10,000 lbs of VCM, it was required to comply with the OSHA PSM Standard (29 CFR 1910.119).

[41] Formosa-IL reported to the IEPA in 2004 that it stores 2.3 million pounds of vinyl chloride and 185,000 pounds of vinyl acetate.

- Incident Investigation—1910.119(m). (Section 4.2); and

- Emergency Planning and Response—1910.119(n).[42] (Section 4.5).

5.2   EPA Regulations

VCM is regulated under the Risk Management Program, and at the time of this incident, it was regulated

as an HAP under the Clean Air Act, National Emissions Standards for Hazardous Air Pollutants

(NESHAP).[43] IEPA oversees compliance with these regulations at the Formosa-IL facility.

5.2.1   Risk Management Program

The Risk Management Program focuses on potential environmental and health hazards outside facility

boundaries. The program requires regulated facilities to develop and implement appropriate risk

management programs to minimize the frequency and severity of chemical plant accidents, and to submit

a Risk Management Plan (RMP) to the EPA identifying, among other things, the chemicals and quantities

stored at the facility, the worst case release scenarios, and the alternative case release scenario.[44] The

Risk Management Program largely incorporates the OSHA PSM requirements for high hazard facilities.

5.2.2   National Emissions Standards for Hazardous Air Pollutants (NESHAP)

Until June 2004, the EPA regulated PVC manufacturing under 40 CFR 63 Subpart J, *National Emission

Standards for Hazardous Air Pollutants for Polyvinyl Chloride and Copolymers Production.*[45] This

regulation required PVC manufacturing facilities that used greater than 10,000 pounds of vinyl chloride

---

[42] This section of the PSM standard references two other OSHA regulations: 1910.120 and 1910.38.

[43] See Section 112 of the CAA, 42 USC 7401 et seq. (1990).

[44] The alternative case release is considered more realistic than the worst case and therefore more likely to occur.

[45] On June 18, 2004, the U.S. Court of Appeals for the D.C. Circuit vacated this regulation and told the EPA to "…reconsider or properly explain its methodology for regulating HAPs emitted in PVC production…." *See* Mossville Environmental Action Now and Sierra Club v. EPA, 370 F.3d 1232 (D.C. Cir. 2004).

(or other listed chemicals) to control emissions by applying the "maximum achievable control technology" (MACT) to the manufacturing process to minimize emissions.[46]

5.2.3   EPA Best Practices Guide for the PVC Industry

In 2002, the EPA Region 3 Office of Enforcement, Compliance, and Environmental Justice embarked on a new enforcement approach to identify specific industries for inspections based on the findings and recommendations of an EPA investigation team of toxicologists, engineers, and scientists. The resulting industry list included the PVC industry for its emission of vinyl chloride.

In 2003, the EPA Region 3 office in Philadelphia, Pennsylvania, began the Vinyl Chloride Pilot Project, gathering and consolidating information on the PVC industry and inspecting PVC plants in Region 3 (Pennsylvania, Delaware, West Virginia, Maryland, and the District of Columbia). In April 2004, the pilot project was expanded to include PVC manufacturing facilities nationwide. Through December 2005, the EPA assessed the air, water, and solid waste compliance status of 83 percent of PVC manufacturing facilities. In addition to collecting information on the industry and inspecting PVC plants, the project planned to develop a PVC industry best practices guide.

6.0 Key Findings

1. Borden Chemical did not implement 1992 PHA recommendations that suggested revisions to policies, procedures, and hardware for the reactor bottom valve interlock bypass to reduce the potential for deliberate or accidental misuse.

2. When it bought Formosa-IL, FPC USA implemented a new organizational structure and reduced staffing. Formosa-IL did not analyze the safety impact of this change.

---

[46] See 67 FR 45885, "Rule for Polyvinyl Chloride and Copolymers Production."

3. In February 2004, an operator inadvertently transferred the contents of an operating reactor, resulting in a VCM release to the atmosphere. Although Formosa-IL recommended that the system be redesigned to prevent inadvertent reactor transfers by April 1, 2004, the redesign was never completed.

4. The interlock for the reactor D310 bottom valve had been bypassed and the drain valve opened, which released the reactor contents into the reactor building.

5. Neither Borden Chemical nor Formosa-IL analyzed the reactor cleaning procedure to identify hazards and recommend safeguards to prevent personnel from draining the wrong reactor during cleaning.

6. Operators on the lower level had no means (indication or communication) to determine the operating status of a reactor from the lower level.

7. Even though the operators were not authorized to use the reactor bottom valve interlock bypass, they had uncontrolled access, and the bypass could be used without detection.

8. The Formosa-IL plant had no written procedure to ensure that safeguards were sufficient to control the risk of a given hazard.

9. FPC USA had previous incidents at Baton Rouge and Formosa-IL similar to the April 23, 2004, Formosa-IL incident. FPC USA did not recognize the similarities among these incidents and make the installation of a more effective bottom valve interlock an urgent priority.

10. More than a year after the Formosa-IL incident, a similar incident occurred at the Delaware City plant indicating that, even after the April 23, 2004, incident, FPC USA had still not instituted rigorous safeguards to prevent an individual from inadvertently opening a reactor bottom valve.

11. Formosa-IL had vague and conflicting procedures for responding to a large VCM release.

12. The Engineering and Safety offices were located close enough to the process to be heavily damaged in the incident.

13. NFPA 15 (NFPA, 2001) provides no clear engineering design basis, including limitations, for water spray deluge systems intended to prevent or mitigate fires and explosions.

7.0   Root and Contributing Causes

7.1   Root Causes

The investigation identified the following root causes:

1. Borden Chemical did not adequately address the potential for human error:

   a) Borden Chemical did not implement 1992 process hazard analysis (PHA) recommendations to change the reactor bottom valve interlock bypass to reduce potential misuse.

   b) In a 1999 PHA, Borden identified severe consequences for opening the reactor bottom valve on an operating reactor, but accepted the interlock, controlled by procedures and training, as a suitable safeguard.

2. Formosa-IL did not adequately address the potential for human error:

   a) After a 2003 incident at FPC USA's Baton Rouge facility, Formosa-IL did not recognize that a similar incident could occur at the Illiopolis facility or take action to prevent it.

   b) Formosa-IL site management did not implement corrective actions identified in the investigation of a similar incident in February 2004 at Formosa-IL.

3. Formosa-IL relied on a written procedure to control a hazard with potentially catastrophic consequences.

7.2   Contributing Causes

The investigation identified the following contributing causes:

1. FPC USA did not have written guidelines for matching safeguards with risk.

2. FPC USA did not have comprehensive written standards managing interlocks at its PVC facilities.

3. FPC USA did not recognize and address common elements of among several serious incidents at its PVC facilities.

4. Formosa-IL employees were unprepared for a major VCM release.

8.0   Recommendations

The CSB makes recommendations based on the findings and conclusions of its investigations. Recommendations are made to parties that can affect change to prevent future incidents, which may include the facility where the incident occurred, the parent company, trade organizations responsible for developing good practice guidelines, regulatory bodies, and/or organizations that have the ability to broadly communicate lessons learned from the incident, such as trade associations and labor unions.

Formosa USA

04-10-I-IL-R1   Review the design and operation of FPC USA manufacturing facilities and implement policies and procedures to ensure that

- Site-wide policies are implemented to address necessary steps and approval levels required to bypass safety interlocks and other critical safety systems.

- Chemical processes are designed to minimize the likelihood and consequences of human error that could result in a catastrophic release.

- Safety impacts of staffing changes are evaluated.

- Risks identified during hazard analyses and near-miss and incident investigations are characterized, prioritized, and that corrective actions are taken promptly.

- High-risk hazards are evaluated using layers of protection analysis (LOPA) techniques and that appropriate safeguards are installed to reduce the likelihood of a catastrophic release of material.

- All credible consequences are considered in near-miss investigations.

- Emergency procedures clearly characterize emergency scenarios, address responsibilities and duties of responders, describe evacuation procedures, and ensure adequate training. Ensure that periodic drills are conducted.

- The siting of offices for administrative and support personnel is evaluated to ensure the safety of personnel should an explosion or catastrophic release occur.

04-10-I-IL-R2   Conduct periodic audits of each FPC USA PVC manufacturing facility for implementation of the items in Recommendation R1. Develop written findings and recommendations. Track and promptly implement corrective actions arising from the audit. Share audit findings with the workforce at the facilities and the FPC USA Board of Directors.

04-10-I-IL-R3   Design and implement a program requiring audits of newly acquired facilities that address the issues highlighted in this report. Document, track, and promptly address recommended actions arising from the audits.

04-10-I-IL-R4   Communicate the contents of this report to all employees of FPC USA PVC facilities.

National Fire Protection Association

04-10-I-IL-R5   Revise NFPA 15, *Standard for Water Spray Fixed Systems for Fire Protection*, to provide additional design guidance for deluge systems designed to prevent or mitigate fires and explosions. Include information concerning the limitations of using deluge systems for this purpose.

Vinyl Institute

04-10-I-IL-R6 Issue a safety alert to your membership highlighting the need to identify design features that may render processes vulnerable to human error and to implement sufficient layers of protection to minimize the likelihood human error causing catastrophic releases of hazardous material. Include lessons from PVC industry industrial accidents (including those described in this report and others highlighted in *The Encyclopedia of PVC* and elsewhere) that involved human error.

Environmental Protection Agency

04-10-I-IL-R7 Ensure that the EPA's Enforcement Alert concerning PVC facilities includes the causes and lessons learned from this investigation. Emphasize the importance of analyzing human factors and the need to implement adequate safeguards to minimize the likelihood and consequences of human error that could result in catastrophic incidents.

AIChE Center for Chemical Process Safety

04-10-I-IL-R8 Develop guidelines for auditing chemical process safety at newly acquired facilities. Emphasize the identification of major hazards, a review of the acquired facility's previous incident history and hazard analyses, the adequacy of management safety systems, and harmonization of the acquired facility's standards and practices with those of the acquiring company.

By the

U.S. Chemical Safety and Hazard Investigation Board

       Carolyn W. Merritt

       Chair

       John S. Bresland

       Member

       Gary L. Visscher

       Member

       William B. Wark

       Member

       William E. Wright

       Member

Date of Board Approval

9.0 References

Agency for Toxic Substances and Disease Registry (ATSDR), 1997. "Dioxin and Dioxin-Like Compounds in Soil, Part 1, ATSDR Interim Policy Guideline," *Toxicology and Industrial Health*, Vol. 13, No. 6, pp. 759-768, 1997.

ATSDR. ToxFAQs, February 1999, http://www.astdr.cdc.gov/facts104.html (accessed August 2006).

Anderson, M., 1999. *IChemE Safety and Loss Prevention Subject Group Newsletter*, Spring 1999.

Bird, F. E. and Germain, G. L., 1985. *Practical Loss Control Leadership*, International Loss Control Institute, Inc.

Center for Chemical Process Safety (CCPS), 2003. *Guidelines for Fire Protection in Chemical, Petrochemical, and Hydrocarbon Processing Facilities*, American Institute of Chemical Engineers (AIChE).

CCPS, 2001. *Layer of Protection Analysis*, AIChE.

CCPS, 1997. *Guidelines for Postrelease Mitigation Technology in the Chemical Process Industry*, AIChE.

CCPS, 1995a. *Guidelines for Safe Process Operations and Maintenance*, AIChE.

CCPS, 1995b. *Guidelines for Technical Planning for On-site Emergencies*, AIChE.

CCPS, 1993. *Guidelines for Safe Automation of Chemical Processes*, AIChE.

CCPS, 1992. *Guidelines for Hazard Evaluation Procedures*, AIChE.

CCPS, 1989. *Guidelines for Technical Management of Chemical Process Safety*, AIChE.

Chemical Manufacturers Association, (CMA) (n.d.), *Management of Safety and Health During Organization Change*.

CMA, 1990. *A Manager's Guide to Reducing Human Errors.*

Crawley, F., Preston, M., and Tyler, B. 2000. *IChemE HAZOP Guide to Best Practice,* Institution of Chemical Engineers.

Dunbobbin, B.R., Paxton, C. L., Peters, G.A., and Dennehy, M.A., 2006. "Preventing Incidents at Newly Acquired Facilities: Implementation of Lessons Learned." *Process Safety Progress,* Vol. 25, No. 1, pp. 64-70.

Hopkins, A., 2005. *Safety, Culture and Risk The Organisational Causes of Disasters*, Sydney, Australia. CCH Australia Limited.

Kletz, T., 1991. *An Engineer's View of Human Error*, Rugby, U.K.: Institution of Chemical Engineers (IChemE).

Lees, F. P., 1996. "Pressure System Design" in *Loss Prevention in the Process Industries: Hazard Identification, Assessment and Control*, Vol. 1, Butterworth-Heinemann.

Lorenzo, D. K., 1990. *A Manager's Guide to Reducing Human Errors: Improving Human Performance in the Chemical Industry*, Chemical Manufacturers Association, Inc.

Nass, L.I., ed., 1976. *Encyclopedia of PVC*, Marcel Dekker, Inc.

National Fire Protection Association (NFPA), 2002. *National Fire Alarm Code*, NFPA 72.

NFPA, 2002a. *Standard for the Inspection, Testing, and Maintenance of Water-Based Fire Protection Systems*, NFPA 25.

NFPA, 2001. *Standard for Water Spray Fixed Systems for Fire Protection*, NFPA 15.

"Product Focus: Polyvinyl Chloride," *Chemical Week*, Vol. 167, No. 42, 14 December 2005, p. 27.

Norman, D.A., 1988. *The Psychology of Everyday Things.*

Perry, R.H. and D.W. Green, 1984. *Perry's Chemical Engineer's Handbook*, 6th ed., McGraw-Hill, Inc.

Sanders, M.S. and E. J. McCormick, 1993. *Human Factors in Engineering and Design*, McGraw-Hill, Inc.

Skelton, B., 1997. *IChemE Process Safety Analysis, An Introduction*, Institution of Chemical Engineers.

Strauch, B., 2002. *Investigating Human Error: Incidents, Accidents, and Complex Systems*, Ashgate.

Thomas, G.O., September 2000. "On the Conditions Required for Explosion Mitigation by Water Sprays," *Process Safety and Environmental Protection*, Vol. 78, Part B.

U.S. Environmental Protection Agency (USEPA), 2003. "Exposure and Human Health Reassessment of 2,3,7,8-Tetrachlorodibenzo-*p*-Dioxin (TSDD) and Related Compounds," EPA/600/P-00/001Cb, December 2003.

USEPA, April 5, 2005. Air Toxics Website, http://www.epa.gov/ttn/atw/, (accessed December 2005).

USEPA, 1982. *Vinyl Chloride- A Review of National Emission Standards*, Office of Air Quality Planning and Standards, February 1982.

Appendix A: Casual Factor Diagram

History of reactor pressure gauge malfunction that keeps bottom valve closed

Operators felt that quick connects were needed for emergency situations

Could not verify reactor pressure from basement level

Incident investigation recommendation not resolved

No radios or other communication with other operators/ supervisors

Quick connect bypass system allows personnel to bypass bottom valve interlock

Reactor/control panel layout identical

Supervisors not readily available

Several possible failure mechanisms

Several possible ignition sources

| D306 empty, NLB in, ready to drain | **CAUSAL FACTOR *** Operator goes to D310 instead of D306 | **CAUSAL FACTOR *** Operator uses emergency hoses to bypass D310 bottom valve | Bottom valve and drain valve open on D310 | VCM and PVC release from open drain on reactor D310 | Deluge system fails to activate in PVC1 | **CAUSAL FACTOR *** Employees stay at the reactor to stop the release | Flammable vapor cloud contacts ignition source | Series of explosions | 5 fatalities, 3 hospitalizations, property damage, community evacuation |

Reactors and control panel labeled

Only supervisors authorized to override BV

Dump-to-drain valve may have been opened before or after bottom valve

Operators did not follow all parts of emergency evacuation plan (e.g., no air-line respirators)

If reactor sits, pressure can creep back up above 10 psi

No group leaders in Formosa organization

* Causal factors are key negative events or negative conditions that, if eliminated, would have prevented a loss event or reduced its effects. Causal factors are used to determine root and contributing causes.

Appendix B: Logic Diagram

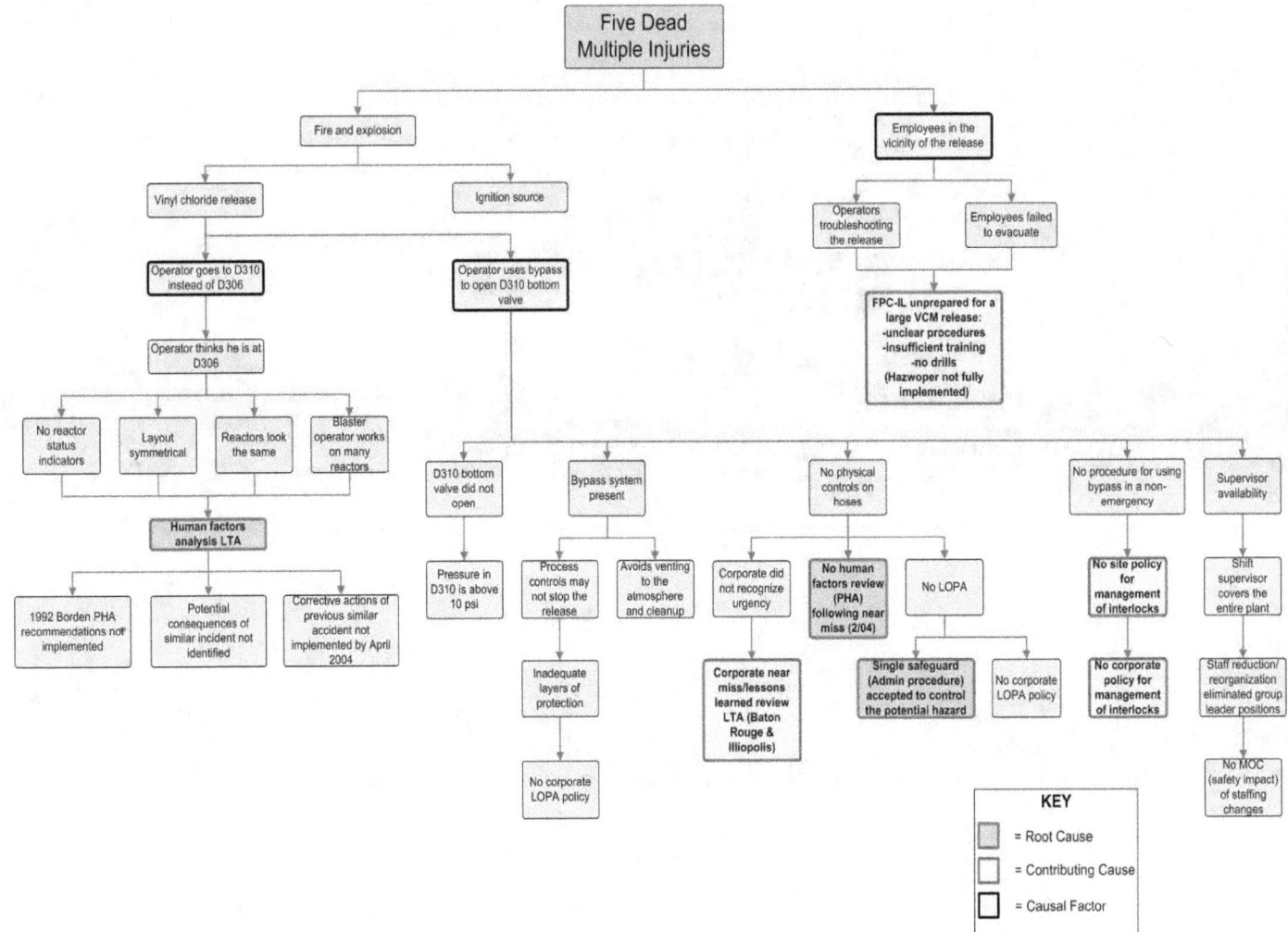

APPENDIX C: Studies of Human Error in the Chemical Process Industries (CPI)

Study	Results
Garrison (1989)	Human error accounted for $563 million of major chemical accidents up to 1984
Joshchek (1981)	80-90% of all accidents in the CPI due to human error
Rasmussen (1989)	Study of 190 accidents in CPI facility; top four causes: • Insufficient knowledge 34% • Design errors 32% • Procedure errors 24% • Personnel errors 16%
Butikofer (1986)	Accidents in petrochemical and refinery units • Equipment and design failures 41% • Personnel and maintenance failures 41% • Inadequate procedures 11% • Inadequate inspection 5% • Other 2%
Uehara and Hoosegow (1986)	Human error accounted for 58% of the fire accidents in refineries • Improper management 12% • Improper design 12% • Improper materials 10% • Misoperation 11% • Improper inspection 19% • Improper repair 9% • Other errors 27%
Oil and Insurance Association Report on Boiler Studies (1971)	Human error accounted for 73% and 67% of total damage for boiler start-up and online explosions, respectively.

(CCPS, 1994)

APPENDIX D: Health Effects of VCM

The health effects of acute (short-term) airborne exposure to high levels of VCM consist mainly of central nervous system depression and irritation of the eyes and respiratory tract. Acute human exposure to extremely high levels of vinyl chloride can cause loss of consciousness, lung and kidney irritation, and can inhibit blood clotting.

Chronic (long-term) exposure to VCM can result in central and peripheral nervous system effects,[47] liver damage, numbness, discomfort in the hands and feet,[48] joint and muscle pain, disfigurement of the extremities, and skin hardening.[49]

Inhaled VCM can increase the risk of a rare form of liver cancer (angiosarcoma). The EPA has classified vinyl chloride as a "Group A, Human Carcinogen,"[50] and the International Agency for Research on Cancer (IARC), part of the World Health Organization (WHO), classifies VCM as a "Group 1" human carcinogen.[51]

---

[47] Central nervous system effects include dizziness, drowsiness, fatigue, headache, visual and/or hearing disturbances, memory loss, and sleep disturbances. Peripheral nervous system effects include burning, pain, tingling, numbness, and weakness in the fingers.

[48] Chronic exposure to VCM can cause some of the symptoms associated with Raynaud's Syndrome due to peripheral nervous system damage, including pain, cyanosis, and cold fingers and toes.

[49] These symptoms are referred to as scleroderma-like skin changes, which, when advanced, can impair circulation and distort the extremities.

[50] The EPA uses this group only when sufficient evidence from epidemiologic studies supports a causal association between exposure to an agent and cancer.

[51] This category is used by IARC when sufficient evidence exists of a cause-and-effect relationship between exposure to the material and cancer in humans. Such determination requires evidence from epidemiologic (demographic and statistical); clinical; and/or tissue/cell studies involving humans exposed to the substance in question.

The OSHA permissible exposure limit (PEL) for VCM is 1 ppm averaged over an 8-hour workday. For shorter exposures to higher concentrations, OSHA has adopted a short-term exposure limit not to exceed 15 minutes at 5 ppm. In addition, employers are required to take certain actions (conduct medical surveillance and periodically monitor worker exposures) when employee exposures are 0.5 ppm or higher averaged over an 8-hour workday.[52]

---

[52] See 29 CFR 1910.1017, *Vinyl Chloride*.

Appendix E: Dioxins

Waste incinerators, forest fires, and backyard burn barrels are all significant sources of dioxin in the environment. Dioxins are also produced when PVC burns, as in the fires after the explosion at Formosa-IL. A fact sheet about dioxins can be found at the Agency for Toxic Substances and Disease Registry (ATSDR) website: http://www.atsdr.cdc.gov/tfacts104.html.

According to the Agency for Toxic Substances and Disease Registry (ATSDR), "dioxin" is a general term that describes a group of 75 chemically related chlorine-containing organic chemical compounds known as chlorinated dibenzo-p-dioxins (CDD). One of the most toxic of these compounds, 2,3,7,8-tetrachlorodibenzo-p-dioxin, or TCDD, has been linked to severe health effects, and is considered a human carcinogen by the WHO and the IARC (ATSDR, 1999). Dioxins break down slowly and are very difficult to remove from the environment.

www.ingramcontent.com/pod-product-compliance
Lightning Source LLC
Chambersburg PA
CBHW081614170526
45166CB00009B/2962